Tuning In

This book can be read from beginning to e[...]
more appropriate to read selected sections [...]
together as a group, using the teaching no[...]
three sections between pairs of children an[...]
write down some questions they would like to have answered
about bikes. They should then look in their sections for answers,
and write them down. Support the children as they read, using
the notes. Then finish the session by drawing the group back
together and asking the children what facts they have learned.

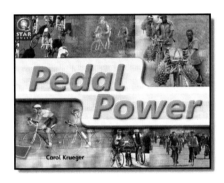

The front cover

Why do you think the book is called 'Pedal Power'?

What differences can you find between the bikes on the cover? (*size, handlebars, tyres, etc*)

Who are wearing helmets? Why?

The back cover

What does the blurb tell us?

Does it make you want to read more about bikes?

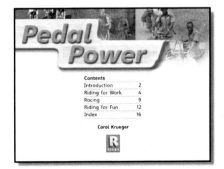

Contents

What are the three main sections going to be about?

What page is the index on?

What kinds of questions might you find answered in this book?

1

Read pages 2 and 3

Purpose: to locate the captions, and recognise different ways of presenting text.

Pause at page 3

Find the names of the following countries: China, Holland, Africa.

Which country would you like to ride a bicycle in? Why?

Why do you think these people are using their bikes?

What did the 'Cycle facts' box tell us?

What new things have you learned? Did any of them answer your questions?

Introduction

Around the world, many people ride bicycles.

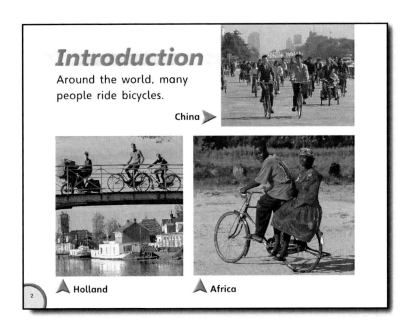

China ▶

▲ Holland   ▲ Africa

2

People use bicycles for work, they ride bicycles in races and they ride bicycles for fun.

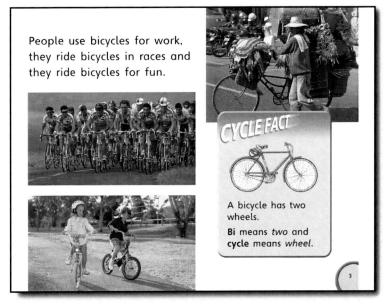

CYCLE FACT

A bicycle has two wheels.

Bi means *two* and **cycle** means *wheel*.

3

3

READ

Read pages 4 and 5

Purpose: to find out how people use their bicycles
for work.

EXPLORE

Pause at page 5

Look at the illustrations. What do you think the people
are doing?

Who can find the words 'cities', 'busy', 'mail'? What do
you think they mean?

Tricky word (page 4):
The word 'Australia' may be beyond the children's
word recognition skills. Tell this word to
the children.

4

Riding for Work

In some cities, people ride bicycles to pick up and deliver packages. Bikes can be faster than cars on busy streets.

Here is someone in Australia ▶ delivering the mail by bike.

◀ Here are some people in Africa carrying bananas to market by bike.

READ

Read pages 6 and 7

Purpose: to find out what tricycles are and what they are used for.

EXPLORE

Pause at page 7

Look at the fact box. What sort of a cycle is illustrated?

Why do you think the man on page 6 needs a tricycle?

What is unusual about the tricycles on pages 6 and 7?

What is a taxi tricycle called?

Where do you think you would see rickshaws?

(Praise the children who read 'rickshaw' accurately, and help other children to use their phonic knowledge to read the word.)

Tricky word (page 7):
The word 'countries' may be beyond the children's word recognition skills. Tell this word to the children.

6

Some people sell things from their bicycles.

Here is someone selling ice cream from his tricycle. The tricycle has a freezer box on the front wheels that keeps the ice cream cold.

CYCLE FACT

A tricycle has three wheels.

Tri means *three* and **cycle** means *wheel*.

In some countries, a tricycle can be a taxi.

This taxi tricycle is called a rickshaw.

CYCLE FACT

People paint their rickshaws with beautiful patterns so they will stand out in the traffic.

READ

Read pages 8 and 9

Purpose: to find out how some children travel to school in India.

EXPLORE

Pause at page 9

Look at the first photograph on page 8. What is on the back of the bike?

What is the name for this kind of bike?

Where do you think the children are going?

▲ Here are some children going to school by rickshaw.

8

Racing

Some bicycles are made for racing.

▲ a mountain bike   ▲ a racing bike

9

READ

Read pages 10 and 11

Purpose: to find out if the questions posed before reading are answered by the text.

EXPLORE

Pause at page 11

What did you want to know about racing bikes?

What have you learnt from this text?

What do you still want to find out?

(Find the word 'triathlon' in the fact box on page 11. Help the children to decode the word and explain that it is a race where the racers have to do three different things.)

Can anyone tell us why racers lean forward when they are racing?

Tricky word (page 10):
The word 'designed' may be beyond the children's word recognition skills. Tell this word to the children.

Racing bikes are faster than other bicycles. They are light and are designed for speed.

Mountain bikes are strong. People ride mountain bikes up hills and across country where other bicycles can't go.

Read pages 12 and 13

Purpose: to look at the different ways in which text
is presented.

Pause at page 13

What is the heading on this page?

Which is the smallest bicycle and who is riding it?

Look at the fact box on page 13. Who can read the first
sentence out loud?

The diagram in the fact box is of a unicycle. What do
you think 'uni' means?

How would you label the diagram?

Read the text on your own and find out why a bike with
only one wheel is called a unicycle.

Riding for Fun

People also ride bicycles for fun.

Here is a clown riding a tiny bicycle.

CYCLE FACT

A unicycle has only one wheel.

Uni means *one* and **cycle** means *wheel*.

Here is a clown riding a unicycle.

READ

Read pages 14 and 15

Purpose: to find out about the longest bike in
the world.

EXPLORE

Pause at page 15

How many people do you think are riding on this bike?

What do you notice about the wheels on this bike?

Look at the sentence on page 15. What do you think
the dash is telling the reader to do?

What two facts have you found out about this bike?

READ

Read page 16

Purpose: to use an index, and recognise its
alphabetical order.

EXPLORE

Pause at page 16

Is this index in alphabetical order?

Why does Africa come before Australia?

Which pages will tell us about racing bikes?

Lots of people can ride this bicycle because it is the longest bicycle in the world.

It was made in Italy.
Nearly forty people can ride it – but it's hard to go round a corner.

Index

After Reading
Revisit and Respond

- This text is a report. What features of a report did you notice? *(sections can be read in any order, it tells us about all the different uses of bikes, not just about one person's bike)*

- What were the most interesting things you learnt about bikes?

- What is the difference between a unicycle, a bicycle and a tricycle?

- Choose some sentences from the book and read the words out of order. Ask the group to tell you the correct order. *(e.g. bicycles made are racing for some, p9)*

- Look at the following words: 'bicycle' (page 2), 'pedal' (cover), 'wheel' (page 3). Tell the group to study the word, chant the names of the letters and then to write down the word from memory.